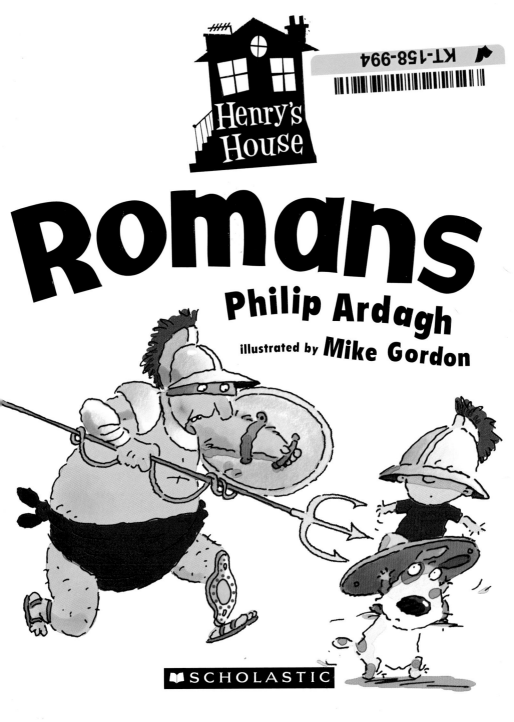

Henry's House

Romans

Philip Ardagh

illustrated by **Mike Gordon**

SCHOLASTIC

**For Freddie, with happy memories of trips
to Roman amphitheatres!**

P.A.

Consultant: Dr Mike Galer

Editorial Director: Lisa Edwards
Senior Editor: Jill Sawyer

Scholastic Children's Books,
Euston House, 24 Eversholt Street,
London NW1 1DB, UK
a division of Scholastic Ltd
London ~ New York ~ Toronto ~ Sydney ~ Auckland
Mexico City ~ New Delhi ~ Hong Kong

First published in the UK by Scholastic Ltd, 2010

Printed and bound by Tien Wah Press Pte. Ltd, Singapore

10 9 8 7 6 5 4 3 2 1

Philip Ardagh and Mike Gordon are regular visitors to Henry's House. Philip (the one with the beard) keeps a note of everything that's going on, and even reads a mind or two. Mike (the one without the beard) sketches whatever he sees, however fantastical it may be ... and together they bring you the adventures of Henry, an ordinary boy in an extraordinary house!

Contents

Welcome to Henry's House!

Hi, I'm Henry! Welcome to my house. Anything can happen here and it often does.

I like finding things out, and so does my dog, Mothball...

I like FOOD too!

FISHCAKE

You never know what's behind the next door or just around the corner, but Jaggers the caretaker usually keeps an eye on things.

That's true! I do.

Then there are the guests ... and not all of us are human.

No wonder every day is such a big adventure!

Gladiators!

Big amphitheatres held up to 50,000 spectators.

Romans came here to watch gladiators fight.

Gladiators were usually slaves or prisoners.

There were different kinds of gladiator.

TRIDENT

A RETARIUS didn't wear much armour, but had a long trident and a net, so he could fight from further away.

WEIGHTS AROUND THE EDGE OF THE NET

LONG SHIELD

A MURMILLO had armour, but just a short sword, so he had to fight close up.

A SAMNITE wore lots of armour and fought with a short sword and a large shield.

It's not fair! How come I have to be the Thracian!!!

A THRACIAN had no metal armour and just a round shield and a small sword.

9

The race is on

Chariots went very fast around the circuit.

Racing chariots were pulled by up to four horses.

Riders were often killed or badly hurt in accidents.

Making a splash

This is the *tepidarium*, with a small warm pool in the middle.

Bathers left their clothes in a cloakroom.

Romans did not wash with soap. They covered themselves with oil. Then they scraped it off their skin with a tool called a strigil.

Bathhouses had a steam room, a hot pool, a warm pool and a cold pool.

WOW! Where are the taps?

Where's the bathmat?

13

The city of Rome

THE BEGINNING OF ROME

Legend says that Rome was founded – set up – in 753 BC. That's over 2,760 years ago.

The story goes that baby twins Romulus and Remus were left on a hillside to die. They were rescued and brought up by a wolf.

When they grew up, they decided to build a city but ended up fighting each other. Romulus killed Remus and called the new city "Rome" after his own name.

The city of Rome really grew from lots of different villages on seven different hills, spreading out until they became one big city.

The people were from a tribe called the Latins.

Latin was also the name of the language they spoke and wrote. Many English words we use today come from Latin ones.

Julius Caesar

Julius Caesar was born into a rich, powerful Roman family in 100 BC.

He became a soldier. When he was 20, he was given one of Rome's highest military awards.

Once, he was kidnapped by pirates. When they let him go, he came back with his troops and had them arrested and killed!

By the time he was 32 he was one of the youngest senators.

In 59 BC Caesar became one of the two leaders of Rome. He passed many laws popular with the people.

He fought many great battles and became a hero. But some Romans thought he was getting too powerful. When he beat a famous Roman general called Pompey, Caesar became Rome's only ruler.

In February 44 BC Julius Caesar was made ruler for life. His word was law. On 15th March 44 BC he was killed by a group of Romans which included his friend Brutus.

Empire

 This coin shows the head of Nero. He was emperor when a huge fire swept through Rome in AD 64. It was rebuilt even bigger and even better.

 This crocodile coin was made to celebrate Rome taking over Egypt.

Roman Empire

BRITAIN

GERMANY

FRANCE

ITALY

GREECE

TURKEY

SPAIN

ROME

SYRIA

NORTH AFRICA

EGYPT

WOW! The Romans were just about everywhere!

Toga!

HENRY'S DO-IT-YOURSELF HOMEMADE TOGA

I. Get an OLD white sheet (ASK A GROWN-UP FIRST!) and cut it into half a circle.

II. Hang one side of your toga over your left shoulder.

III. Take the other end in your right hand and pass it under your right arm...

IV. ...and throw it over your left shoulder.

T-SHIRT AS TUNIC

Women didn't wear togas.

Like men, they wore a tunic but with a dress on top.

Men and women wore sandals.

Dresses were simple but colourful.

Citizens and slaves

There were three types of citizen...

RICH CITIZENS

BUSINESSMEN
CITIZENS

ORDINARY CITIZENS
(MOST OF THEM)

Only men could be citizens.

Who are they over there?

Slaves, I'm afraid. They were bought and sold and did hard work for no pay.

Having a slave in Roman times seemed normal. Most Romans didn't think it was wrong.

That's horrible!

Slaves were men, women and children owned by Roman citizens or by Rome itself. Some had cruel masters. Some had nice ones. They worked as servants, farm hands, builders or even as miners.

Some slaves were given their freedom by their masters.

To the forum

You must be Henry! My name is Marcus Septimus.

Why do you have a purple line around your toga, Mr Septimus?

It shows that I'm a senator, a member of the Senate.

The Senate was ancient Rome's parliament, where laws were passed.

Senators were voted for by citizens.

At one time, the Senate ruled Rome. This period was called the Republic.

Later, emperors ruled Rome.

STATUE OF A FAMOUS SENATOR

Why is that statue wearing a skirt?

SLAVE

WINE JARS

Horseplay

A famous emperor, best known as Caligula, once tried to make his horse a consul, which was the top job in the Senate. The senators weren't too pleased about it!

27

Chop! Chop! Shop! Shop!

You and your fine animal must meet my family, Henry.

I must be off, Henry. Your father is having trouble with pirates in the attic.

Fine animal? I LIKE this Marcus Septimus!

Here they are! This is my wife, Claudia, and our children, Lydia and Augustus.

Hello, Henry. Want to come to the market with us?

Augustus is wearing a bulla. A bulla was a good-luck charm always given to children.

He is wearing a tunic. He won't wear a toga until he is much older.

Lydia is wearing a dress called a stolla.

Roman market places were a mixture of open-fronted shops and market stalls.

People lived above the shops.

FURNITURE SHOP

WEAVER'S SHOP

BAKERY STALL

CAFE

FRUIT STALL

No sign of the runaway lion OR any of the runaway slaves.

But I did just spot a roll-away bun!

DROOL! SLURP!

Come on, follow me!

On the road

Shops and stallholders could only bring goods into Rome very early in the morning. Otherwise their carts might block the roads.

Roman farmers kept chickens and geese for eggs and meat.

Pork was the most popular meat.

Romans didn't have sugar. They used honey to sweeten food.

Sheep's milk was a much-loved drink.

Roman roads were very well made. They are famous for being straight.

Many were built by soldiers for soldiers. Good roads meant that armies could move about very quickly.

A route was chosen for a road and cleared of trees and rocks and shrubs.

The top of the road was raised in a curve like this.

DITCH

This bump is called a camber.

Keep up, Mothball!

A one-metre trench was dug and filled with stones and cement.

Rainwater ran off into ditches at either side.

March on!

On the edge of town...

A *centurion* was in charge of each century.

This soldier is a *tesserarius*. He is in charge of passwords.

THE CENTURY'S STANDARD

A CENTURY'S STANDARD-BEARER

Can we stop now? My paws ache!

The road stretches for MILES.

And here comes a whole legion of soldiers!

There's Uncle Severus!

Each legion had a silver eagle. If a legion lost its eagle in battle, the legion was ended.

The eagle was carried by the aquilifer.

LION SKIN

AQUILIFER

LEATHER AND METAL ARMOUR

I love his hat!

A legion was led by a *legatus*.

The army

A **Roman legion** was made up of around 5,500 soldiers. This was divided into:
9 **cohorts** of around 480 men and a double first cohort of 960 men.
A cohort was made up of 6 **centuries** of 80 men each.
A century was made up of 10 **contubernia** of 8 soldiers each.
(To begin with, a century had 100 soldiers in it.)

There were two types of camp. Ones built of stone and ones made of tents, such as this one.

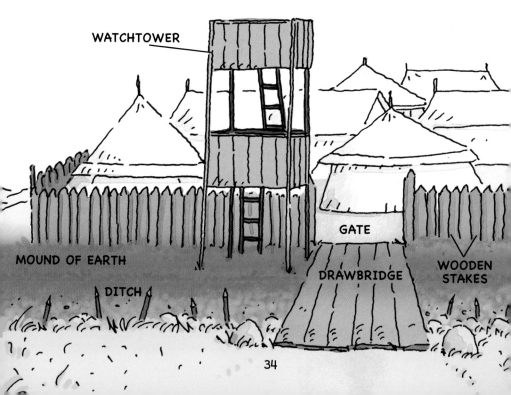

WATCHTOWER

MOUND OF EARTH

DITCH

GATE

DRAWBRIDGE

WOODEN STAKES

Every Roman army camp was laid out in the same way.

When an army was on the march, they would rebuild their tent camp EVERY NIGHT.

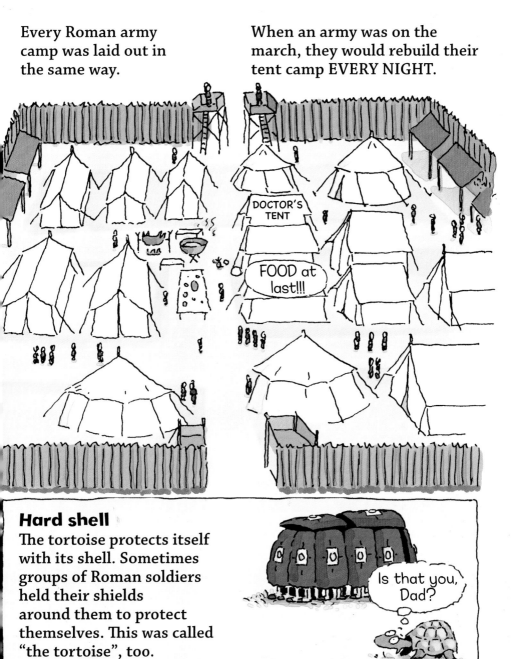

DOCTOR'S TENT

FOOD at last!!!

Hard shell

The tortoise protects itself with its shell. Sometimes groups of Roman soldiers held their shields around them to protect themselves. This was called "the tortoise", too.

Is that you, Dad?

A feast!

Romans' biggest meals were their banquets for the rich.

Banquets used to be just for men. Later, women could come too.

MUSICIAN

FISH

EGGS

SALADS

People ate lying down on couches.

People ate with their fingers (and sometimes with a spoon).

There were up to three people on each couch.

The food and wine was served by slaves.

Bits and pieces

Stop looking at me like that, fish-face!

Wow! Look at this floor. It's made up of tiny little pieces!

It's called a mosaic, Henry. Tiny coloured tiles are used to make amazing pictures and patterns.

The floor was covered in wet plaster and then the tiny tiles were pressed into it.

Some patterns were used all over Rome. Some pictures were only made once.

This mosaic is going to be a "beware of the dog" sign.

HENRY'S DO-IT-YOURSELF MINI-MOSAICS

THE PAPER WAY

1. Draw a nice colourful picture (or cut one out of a comic).

2. Cut it into small squares.

3. Stick it back together (like a jigsaw puzzle) on a piece of cardboard.

LEAVE LITTLE SPACES BETWEEN THE PIECES

THE SQUIDGY WAY

1. Cut out different-coloured squares of cardboard.

2. Roll out a thin layer of playdough.

3. Press the cardboard "tiles" into the playdough to make a pattern or picture.

No place like home

Most Romans living in town rented a flat. Many flats were above shops.

CHEAPEST, SMALLEST FLATS

NICEST, MOST EXPENSIVE FLATS

SHOP

Rich Romans often lived in fine town houses.

They also had country houses called villas.

They didn't have wallpaper but pictures painted straight onto the wall.

Wealthy Romans' homes were rich with ornaments and colours.

It looks like a garden!

Rooms were lit with all kinds of lamps and lanterns.

WICK FOR BURNING FLAME

OIL INSIDE

METAL

LANTERN

CHAINS

GLASS

HANGING LAMP

People living in flats often shared group toilets on the ground floor.

EXCUSE ME!!!

People could sit in a row.

Ye gods!

43

Didn't Romans worship in temples too?

Wait f-f-or me!

Follow me!

Roman temples were copies of ancient Greek ones.

COLUMNS

MUSICIANS

The bull is going to be sacrificed: killed as a "present" to a god as part of a festival.

ZOOM!

ROAR!!!

YIKES!!! Here we go again!

Temples were full of treasure. Rich Romans could keep their gold there – like a bank. It was looked after by priests and priestesses.

A huge statue of the god or goddess was inside the temple.

Romans picked and chose which of the many gods and goddesses to pray to.

Most ceremonies happened outside the temple.

COOL!

Off to school

Boys from rich families went to a school called a *ludus*. They were there from ages six to eleven.

When they were eleven, some boys went on to a school called a *grammatics*.

Many teachers came from Greece.

ROME

GREECE

A SCROLL

This boy's parents have sent a *paedagogus* here, to make sure that he works hard.

ABACUS FOR COUNTING

Sit next to me, Henry. You can write on this wax tablet.

STYLUS FOR WRITING IN WAX

A teacher called a rhetor taught older boys how to speak in public. This would be good if they wanted to be a senator or a lawyer.

Here we are at my house.

Hello, Henry. I've got some friends around to play!

Great! Do you have any doggy snacks?

This girl is playing an instrument called a lyre.

Goodie! I get to sing!

A kind of draughts (or checkers) was a popular game.

WOODEN DOLL

BALL

Sheep's knucklebones were used like jacks or dice.

Doctor! Doctor!

Half an hour later...

Rich Romans paid for doctors to visit them at home.

Very rich Romans had their own private doctors.

Most patients had to go to the doctor if they wanted to see him.

HERBS

SCROLLS

Doctors didn't have to pay taxes if they treated the poor for free.

Women doctors helped mothers have their babies.

Army doctors often had to cut off arms and legs.

Inside an army hospital tent.

STATUE OF AESCULAPIUS, GOD OF MEDICINE

SURGICAL INSTRUMENTS

To the play

Theatres were huge. In the bigger ones 27,000 people could see a play at one time.

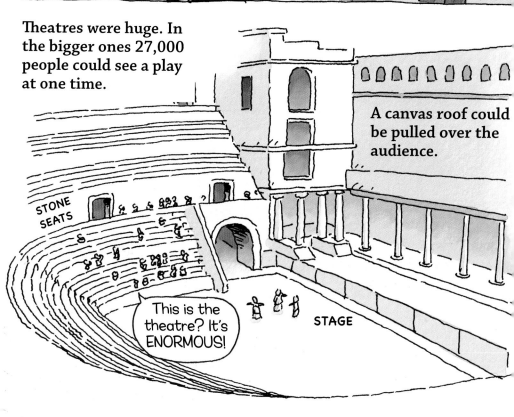

A canvas roof could be pulled over the audience.

STONE SEATS

This is the theatre? It's ENORMOUS!

STAGE

Feeling hot, hot, hot!

57

Timeline

ROMAN NUMBERS

I = 1	XI = 11
II = 2	XIX = 19
III = 3	XX = 20
IV = 4	XXIV = 24
V = 5	XL = 40
VI = 6	XLV = 45
VII = 7	L = 50
VIII = 8	LX = 60
IX = 9	XCIX = 99
X = 10	C = 100

753 BC Legend has it that the City of Rome is founded.

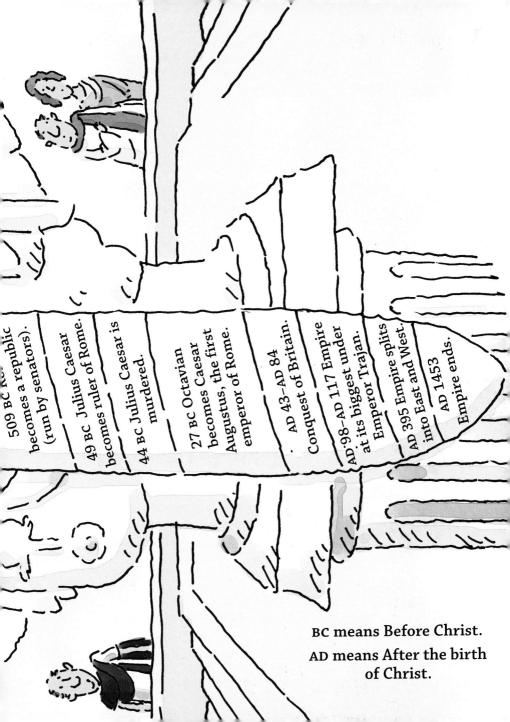

509 BC Rome becomes a republic (run by senators).

49 BC Julius Caesar becomes ruler of Rome.

44 BC Julius Caesar is murdered.

27 BC Octavian becomes Caesar Augustus, the first emperor of Rome.

AD 43–AD 84 Conquest of Britain.

AD 98–AD 117 Empire at its biggest under Emperor Trajan.

AD 395 Empire splits into East and West.

AD 1453 Empire ends.

BC means Before Christ.

AD means After the birth of Christ.

Glossary

Amphitheatre: a huge, round building, like a football stadium, where the Romans went to watch live entertainment.

Chariot: a small, speedy cart, pulled by horses and driven standing up. The driver is called a charioteer.

Fortune-teller: someone who claims that they can look into the future. Romans often paid fortune-tellers to tell them what was going to happen next in their lives.

Gladiators: mostly slaves who were forced to fight animals and each other to entertain people.

Ides: in the Roman calendar, Ides means the fifteenth of March, May, July or October, and the thirteenth day of the other months.

Latin: the language spoken and written in Ancient Rome.

Masks: worn by actors to look like familar characters, easily recognized by members of the audience, however far back they sat.

Paedagogus: a slave who had special responsibility for the son of rich parents. He went with the boy everywhere, even to school, to make sure he worked hard.

Roman Empire: all the countries that were ruled over by the Roman emperor.

Sacrifice: a human or animal that is killed as a "present" to a god.

Senators: the group of men who made the laws in ancient Rome.

Slave: a person "owned" by someone else and forced to work for no money.

Slave trader: someone who buys and sells slaves.

Strigil: a tool used for scraping off bath oils.

Tablet: what schoolchildren used to write on during lessons. In Roman times these were made from wax. Letters and numbers were cut into the wax using a special stick called a stylus. The wax could then be flattened and written into again and again.

Temples: buildings where Romans worshipped their gods.

Tepidarium: the warm room in a Roman bathhouse.

Tesserarius: a soldier who kept watch at night. People could only get past him if they had the correct password.

Index

Henry's House

We hope you enjoyed your visit

to **Henry's House**

Come back soon!

Look out for:
- **Knights and Castles**
- **Creepy-crawlies**
- **Egyptians**
- **Dinosaurs**
- **Bodies**
- **Space**

For more facts and fun, visit us at
www.headforhenryshouse.co.uk